Outside the Box

New Ideas!

Heather E. Schwartz

Publishing Credits

Rachelle Cracchiolo, M.S.Ed., *Publisher*
Conni Medina, M.A.Ed., *Managing Editor*
Nika Fabienke, Ed.D., *Series Developer*
June Kikuchi, *Content Director*
Michelle Jovin, M.A., *Assistant Editor*
Lee Aucoin, *Senior Graphic Designer*

TIME For Kids and the TIME For Kids logo are registered trademarks of TIME Inc. Used under license.

Image Credits: p.23 Photo by Anthony Devlin/TNR Communications; all other images from iStock and/or Shutterstock.

Teacher Created Materials
5301 Oceanus Drive
Huntington Beach, CA 92649-1030
http://www.tcmpub.com
ISBN 978-1-4258-4966-5
© 2018 Teacher Created Materials, Inc.
Printed in Malaysia
Thumbprints.042019

Table of Contents

Break Out of the Box

What does it mean to "think outside the box"? It means to challenge your imagination. Thinking outside the box helps you come up with new solutions. Creative thinking helps you dream up new ideas. It can help you solve problems and **invent** new things.

How do you get started? This book will show you the way.

5

Jump-Start Your Imagination

Do you want to think more creatively? There are lots of tips to try.

Train Your Brain

Moving around gives your brain a break from schoolwork. But that is not all it does. Scientists have found that regular exercise can help your brain think in new and creative ways.

Jump Around

Write three sentences about your day. Then, get up and get active. Now, write three more sentences. Studies show that writing should feel easier after some exercise.

Keep a Journal

It is sometimes easier to be creative when you know no one will see your work. You can create a private journal. That means you do not have to show it to anyone.

What you put in your journal is up to you. You are free to be yourself on every page.

Get Artsy

Grab your crayons, paint, glue, and glitter. Then, get inspired by the world around you.

Draw pictures for a book that you write. Cut up photos to create a **collage**. (Just be sure to get permission first!) Use something old to make something new. You do not have to start from scratch to create original art.

11

Try Something New

Try doing things differently. You might see the world in a whole new way.

Begin with the Background

Draw a picture, but do not draw people or animals at first. Instead, start with the background. Draw details like trees, grass, and the sky. Then, decide where characters fit into the scene you have drawn.

Pick a Pencil

In school, you probably use a #2 pencil. Did you know that pencils come in other numbers? A low number means the **graphite** is soft. It will leave a dark mark on paper. Use #3 or #4 pencils to leave a lighter mark.

2

3

4

5

6

7

8

9

Shake Up Your Routine

Tell your parents or guardians that you want to conduct an experiment for one week. Say you want to do your homework at different times. On the first day, do it right after school. The next day, wait until after dinner. Try other times for the rest of the week. Who knows? You might find that you work better at certain times of the day.

Sleepyhead

Studies show that kids ages 6 to 13 need a lot of sleep. They should sleep 9 to 11 hours each night. When they get less sleep, they may find it hard to focus.

Day

Night

Scan the Shelves

Sometimes, a reader gets stuck in a **rut**. Do you always read the same type of books? Next time you visit a library, try something new. Grab a graphic novel. Pore over some poetry. Flip through a fairy tale. See if you learn any fun facts or new words.

Imagine That!

Scientists have found that novels teach readers new skills. They show readers how it feels to be in another person's place. They give your brain a workout.

MYSTERY   BIOGRAPHY
Adventure Thriller
NONFICTION

Play a Different Way

Hanging out with your friends is fun, but new people can bring fresh ideas to your group. Invite some kids you do not know well to play with you.

When you are by yourself, you can change how you play, too. Use old toys to invent brand-new games.

19

Break Some Rules

Most of the time, you should follow the rules. But these rules are safe to break.

Write a Silly Story

Think of a story that makes you laugh. Write it just for yourself (not for school). Do not worry about spelling or grammar. Do not worry if it is silly, impossible, or does not make sense. Writers **revise** their work to correct their mistakes. You can, too. Just focus on writing down all of your ideas first.

Once ~~upon~~ upon a time, in a land far away, there lived a dragon and a mouse.

Style Yourself

Your clothes can send a message. You can use them to express your creativity. They can help you tell people about yourself. Are you in a goofy mood? Maybe you could wear two different shoes. Or you might want to wear a costume instead of your regular clothes. Go for it!

LEGO Dress

Clothing is not always made of cloth. A famous designer once decorated a dress with LEGO® bricks. She used thousands of pieces!

Start at the End

Try to do things in a different order when you want to be creative. For example, choose a fiction book to read. Flip to the last page or two, and read the ending. Now you know how it turns out, but you can still enjoy reading it from the beginning.

Spoiler Alert

Studies show that knowing how a story ends can make reading more fun. Readers like all parts of stories. If they know how the books will end, readers can focus more on the journeys.

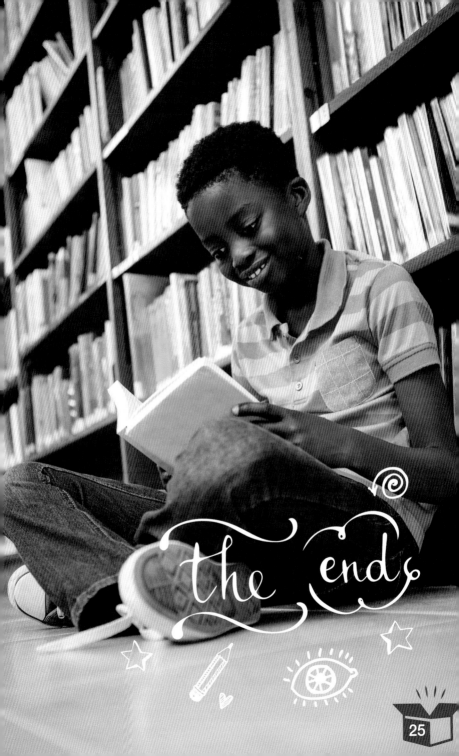

the ends

Focus on Fun

When you think outside the box, you can do practically anything. You can change your life. You can even change the world.

Learning to think more creatively may take practice before it becomes a **habit**. But it is not hard. The best way to get better at it is to keep trying. So have fun and get thinking!

Glossary

collage—a work of art made by attaching pieces of different materials to a flat surface

graphite—a shiny black material used in pencils

habit—a way of behaving that a person does regularly

invent—create or make something for the first time

revise—to make changes to correct and improve something

rut—a situation in which things stay the same for a while